Fifty Pages of Wisdom

Jennifer Foster

Published by Jennifer Foster, 2024.

While every precaution has been taken in the preparation of this book, the publisher assumes no responsibility for errors or omissions, or for damages resulting from the use of the information contained herein.

FIFTY PAGES OF WISDOM

First edition. July 1, 2024.

ISBN: 979-8227202611

Written by Jennifer Foster.

For My Ancestors.

FIFTY PAGES OF *Wisdom*

Advice I wish someone had given me in my twenties

JENNIFER FOSTER

Introduction

At fifty-one years old, I look back and shudder at the thought of how I used to feel, every day, during my twenties and thirties. The amount of anxiety and pressure I felt was immense. I was a young woman, living in the city of Chicago, busting ass trying to pay rent, party and survive. Every day of the week felt forced. I rarely wanted to get up and go to the corporate job I was supposed to feel lucky to have.

"What's it all for?" was a question I often asked myself and others, repeatedly. No one had any answers I wanted to hear.

I hope this book helps you. There are so many messages in it I wish I had read when I was still trying to figure out life.

If you're reading this, know one thing: *you belong here and you are loved.* You belong in this world. You were born here, on this little rock floating through space.

You belong here.

Much Love.

~ Jennifer

it's more than ok
to have limitations

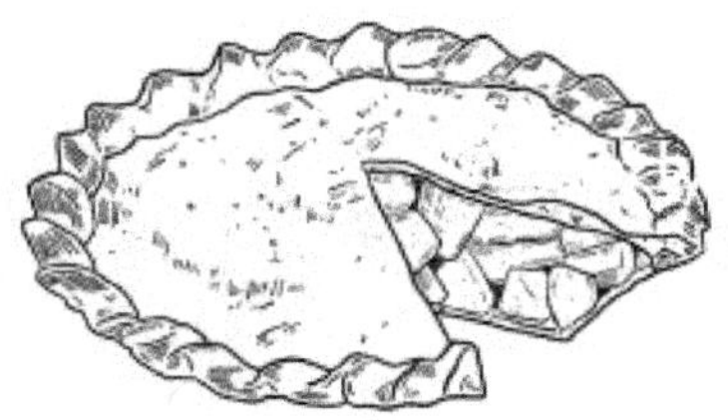

some people can eat an entire pie in 30 seconds.
but you cannot. and that's ok. beating ourselves up
for our limitations is about as smart as a fish beating
itself up for not being able to survive on land.

life does not have to be complicated

people choose
to make life complicated

we could all be living in harmony, planting gardens,
sharing food, learning from one another, and helping one
another thrive on this planet.

we could be picking breakfast, lunch,
and dinner from our immediate environment. for free.
but people want to drive miles and pay for old food instead.

people choose to make life complicated.

your life does not have to be.

without sorrow

we would not know joy

the deeper the sorrow, the greater the joy.

JENNIFER FOSTER

having a partner
can be lonely
too

it's ok to feel lonely. loneliness
is a new plague for human beings.
we cannot always blame loneliness
on those around us.

you do not have to
give birth to a child

in order to be a parent

8

you don't have to
have children

it is not a requirement in life.
many people choose
to not have children
and they don't
end up
in hell.

FIFTY PAGES OF WISDOM

your parents
were never perfect

it's a shock when you first discover they aren't perfect
but they never were
and that feeling of betrayal is strong
that feeling of being duped
the overwhelming disappointment
it's unfair.

it is a pivotal moment of awareness
address it now
or you will still be addressing it
in your 50s and beyond.

no relationship

is perfect

no matter how good it looks from the outside.

maybe
your anxiety
isn't what you think it is

maybe
you're living
in survival mode

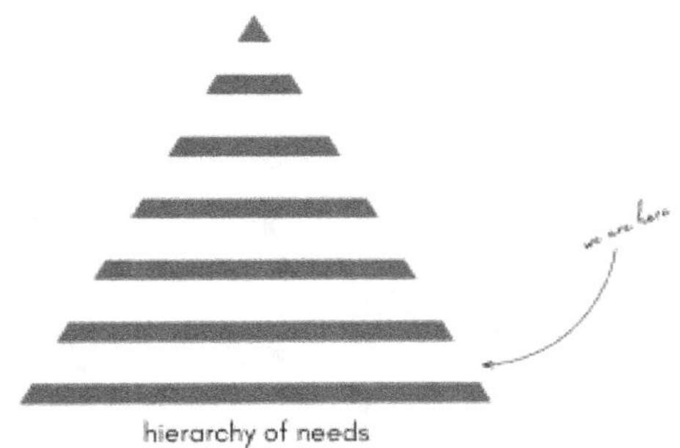

living in survival mode can lead to feelings of anxiety, depression, and burnout. every day tasks may feel more difficult to complete. the stress that comes with survival mode can lead to unhealthy coping mechanisms, strained relationships, resulting in feeling like withdrawing from society. there is a loss of enjoyment in life.

survival mode impacts both the rich and the poor. your mind determines what is at stake.

are you anxiously depressed, or suffering from unnecessary and nonsensical societal pressures and oppression?

there is nothing wrong with *you*.

replace your thoughts
with silence

and you will find out
who you are

you don't meditate
to
quiet your mind

you meditate
to teach yourself

that your thoughts
are a nuisance

you don't need
to think
all the time

you schedule time for breaks. schedule time to *not* think.

stop denying
what you love

you were called to it for a reason.

JENNIFER FOSTER

relationships
do not last
forever

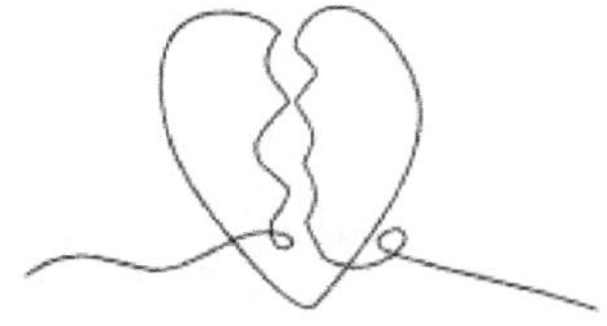

endings always mark new beginnings.
everything evolves. relationships included.
sometimes, a phase needs to end, in order
for something more beautiful
to emerge.

superficial friendships

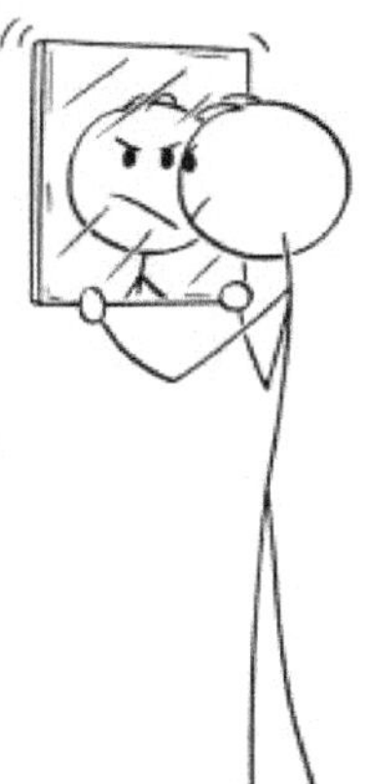

will suck the life out of you

treat your friend search
just like
your life partner search.

most people

show their mask

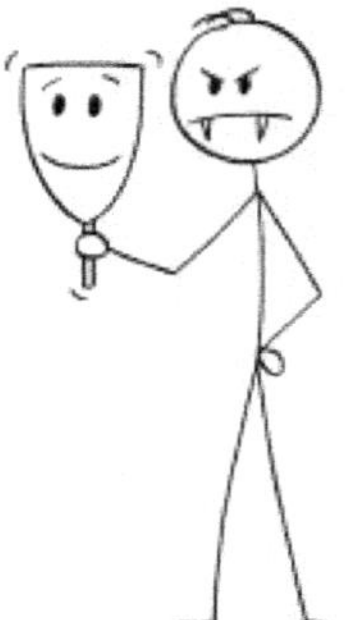

first

be patient.

consider the possibility
of
your mother's pain
being deeper than yours

she did her best.

you don't need validation

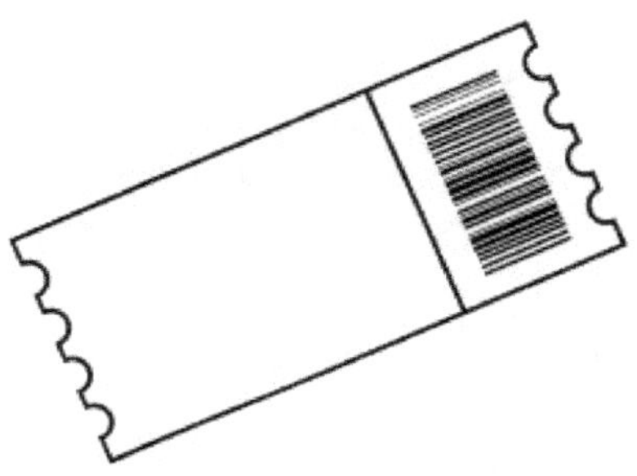

you are not
a parking ticket

healthy validation is great. but most of us don't seek
healthy validation. we seek validation of our divinity
from toxic sources.

if you took away everyday societal pressures and judgments,
what would you have to validate?

when you are five
5 minutes feels like one year

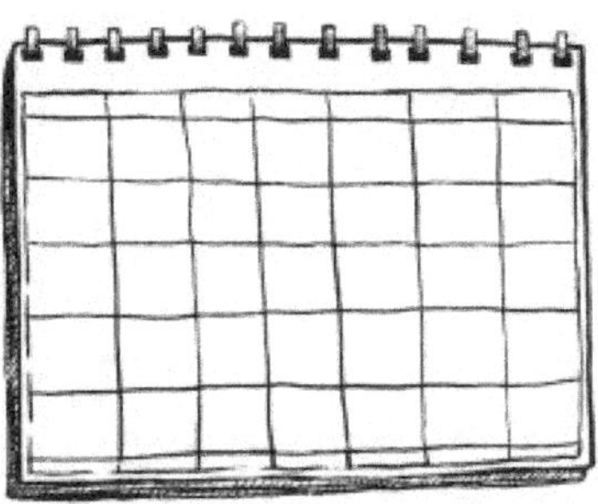

when you are fifty
one year feels like 5 minutes

every moment matters.
every moment is a future memory.

you cannot prove your worth

by having sex

if you think about it, it's kinda silly.
sex is human nature.
you are desirable
by human nature.

maintaining your flexibility
is everything

it allows you to continue to move
in your later years.

JENNIFER FOSTER

be aware of your
death

in the book, Tibetan Book of the Living and Dying,
it is told
monks assume they may not wake up the next day.
each night, in preparation for sleep,
they remain aware of death.

if you live life in this way, when you open your eyes,
each morning,
you will be delighted. delighted to see the light.
delighted to be alive,
at least for one more day.

friends don't always
give the best
advice

our friends are not our therapists.

JENNIFER FOSTER

you don't have to
get married

it is not a requirement.
people live very happy lives
unmarried.
You can live
'happily ever after'
unmarried.

the person who knows what is best for you

is *you*

stay away
from the people
who treat you poorly

break the cycle. it will change the way you view life.

the dream is now
life is now

right now

not next week, next month, next year, or in 2034.
life is happening, now.

your thoughts

are
your biggest
obstacle

success = self-mastery.

you
are
enough

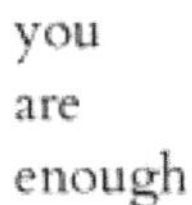

you don't need to prove anything.

humans contemplating
the meaning of life

is like

a dog contemplating
the meaning
of a ball

does it matter?

just because someone is an adult

does not automatically mean
they are smart

they believe it though.

protect the elderly

one day
you will stand
in their shoes

if you disrespect the elderly today
how are you going to feel
when you are their age?

35

you are not

who you think
you are

friends
are family

sometimes, friends are closer than family
and that's ok.

you are aging right now

run, play, experience life

sometimes,
your thoughts
are wrong

just because you have a thought
does not mean
it's true.

music is
the
essence of life

without it, there would be no dancing.

some people say
if you have
"butterflies"
it must be love

but love
is not
uncomfortable

relationships are uncomfortable. loss is uncomfortable.
love, is the foundation of the universe.

41

thoughts
are not
directives

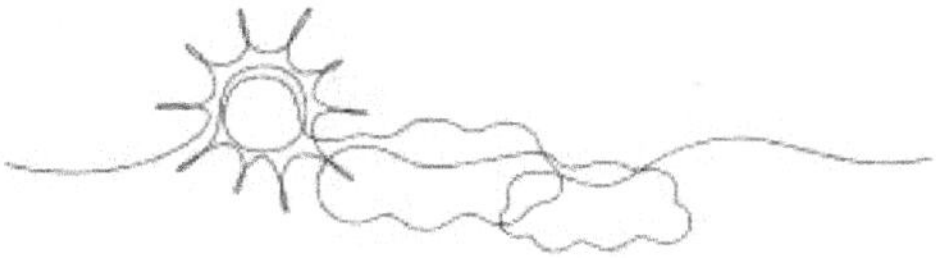

just because you have a thought
does not mean
you must act on it

love
is not
earned

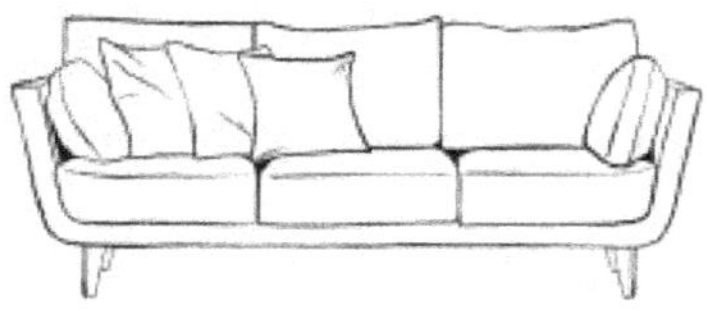

it is
like a comfortable couch
you settle into

love is not a commodity. love isn't a thing.
love cannot be lost.
love is a state of being.

your intuition
is
everything

to abandon your intuition
is to abandon your peace.

if you don't know
your values
other people
will run
your life

whatever you value most,
make sure you are
honoring
that.

your imagination
is
everything

cultivate it, use it
to create the life
of your dreams.

you won't truly
know love

until you
know death

grief is
a gateway

to transformation

the ache
is an invitation
to expansion.

48

everyone you meet is in some kind of
pain.

in 2022, 3.27 million deaths were recorded
in the United States.
this means
millions of people grieve, daily.
millions of people are in pain.

love does not have a type

people have a type

love indiscriminately flows through every
molecule, every body, every species of the universe
and has no limits.

don't confuse
your need
for a life partner

with your need
for happiness

one does not
guarantee the other

seek guidance
seek wisdom

but in the end
you must follow

your own path

JENNIFER FOSTER

it's all made up

beauty standards, relationship rules, gender roles, politics,
capitalism, time, paths to follow, rules, laws, money, state
borders, country borders, religion, your identity, your
own goals, how you think you should be acting,
your sign....all.made.up.

Live Life Your Own Way

Afterward

Many people in your life will try to tell you what is best for you. Many people in your life will disagree with the path you have chosen for yourself. And that's ok! It's not their path. It's yours. They are under the false impression that they can predict your future.

No one knows what the future holds. This fact does not have to create anxiety. The only reason it does, is because we have convinced ourselves that we can predict and control the future. When it doesn't work out, we blame ourselves…in essence, for being ineffective fortune tellers.

Whether we have one life or multiple lives, the only thing we're conscious of is right now. The only moment we actually exist in, is this moment. Yet our awareness prefers to be elsewhere. The future, the past. Anywhere but right now. Anywhere but in silence.

This is the root of suffering.

An unawakened awareness is the shield preventing joy.

The solution to the anxiety? Since we cannot predict the future, the next best thing is to learn how to stay connected to the present. The present holds our power. The present holds our essence.

But if there is one thing I really want you to take away from this book, it's the message that "it's all made up."

I originally heard this message during a training I attended in Chicago for life coaches back in 2007 (Thank you, Rick Tamlyn!). "It's all made up" has stuck with me all this time. When I'm feeling down on myself, judging myself, or thinking I'm a failure, if I can remember, "it's all made up!" then I can shake off the negativity and move on.

It's All Made Up!!

Human beings made up all the rules we follow today. Rules for how we live, relate to one another, love one another, and exist in the world.

Survival is not complicated. Human beings make surviving much more complicated than it actually is.

Your beliefs, thoughts, attitude, personality, views, and opinions of yourself and the world, originated outside of yourself.

So now the question is, do your current beliefs, thoughts, attitude, personality, lifestyle, and the way you live your life, and view yourself…

Does it all feel authentic to you?

Are you comfortable in your own skin?

Do you live most of your life from a space of obligation, or from an empowered space of choice?

If you didn't think you had it already, you now have permission to design your own life, without self-judgment, without guilt. I pray that you allow yourself to experience joy.

Much Love!

~ Jennifer

Don't miss out!

Visit the website below and you can sign up to receive emails whenever Jennifer Foster publishes a new book. There's no charge and no obligation.

https://books2read.com/r/B-A-NBVRB-XPLPD

BOOKS2READ

Connecting independent readers to independent writers.

About the Author

Jennifer Foster is a Life Coach with fifteen years of experience and is the creator of the popular online coaching site, ***Open Your Mind, A School for Unlearning***. The author is currently finishing her master's in clinical counseling and is a licensed Registered Behavior Technician, delivering ABA therapy to children on the spectrum.

The author is known for her unique approach to relationships and well-being, using the "decolonize therapy" approach to healing, believing mental health is largely impacted by systemic inequities, the trauma of oppression, and the evolution of a society built on "grind culture."

Read more at https://jennifer-foster-s-school5.teachable.com/p/home.